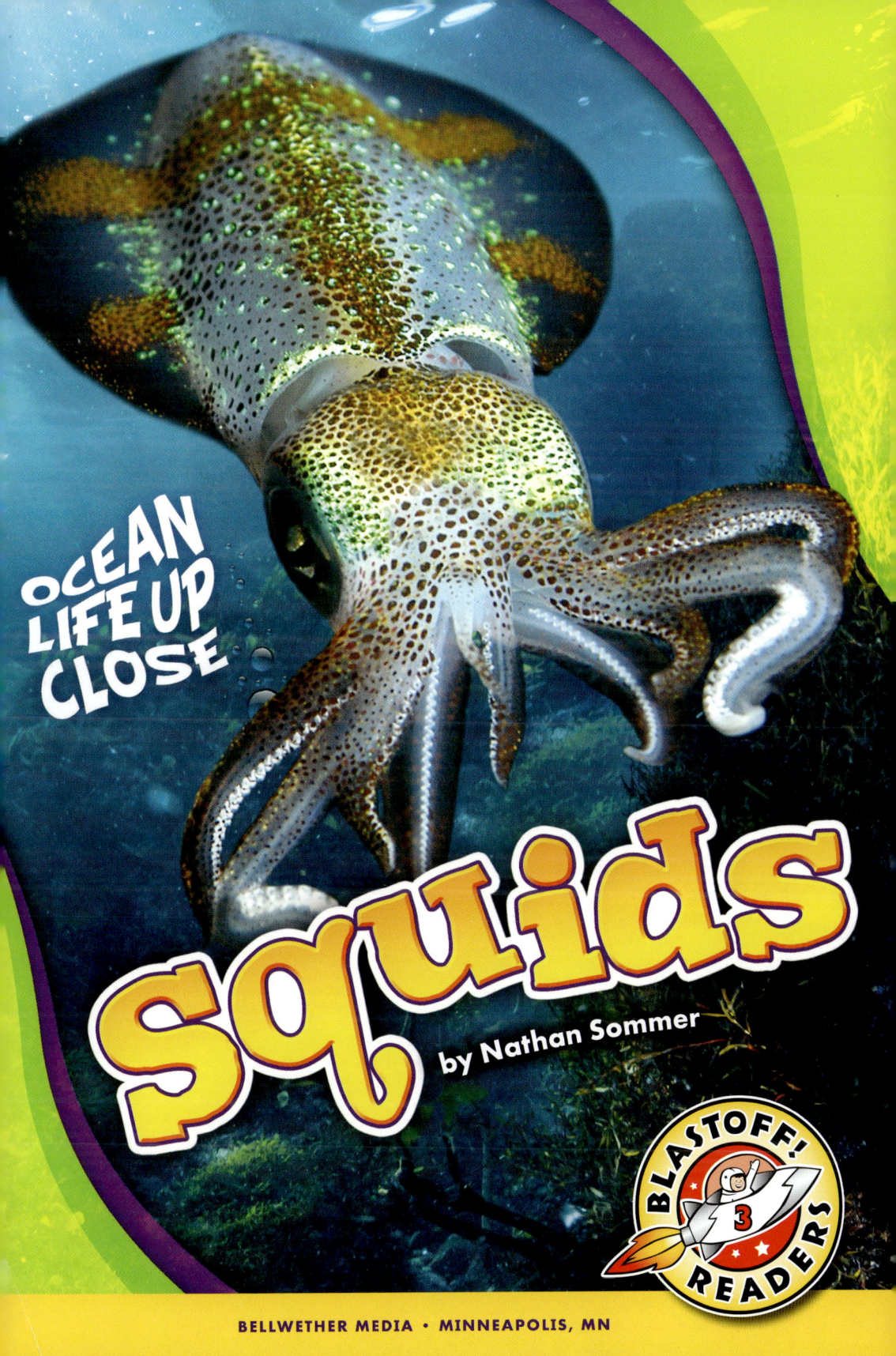

Note to Librarians, Teachers, and Parents:

Blastoff! Readers are carefully developed by literacy experts and combine standards-based content with developmentally appropriate text.

Level 1 provides the most support through repetition of high-frequency words, light text, predictable sentence patterns, and strong visual support.

Level 2 offers early readers a bit more challenge through varied simple sentences, increased text load, and less repetition of high-frequency words.

Level 3 advances early-fluent readers toward fluency through increased text and concept load, less reliance on visuals, longer sentences, and more literary language.

Level 4 builds reading stamina by providing more text per page, increased use of punctuation, greater variation in sentence patterns, and increasingly challenging vocabulary.

Level 5 encourages children to move from "learning to read" to "reading to learn" by providing even more text, varied writing styles, and less familiar topics.

Whichever book is right for your reader, Blastoff! Readers are the perfect books to build confidence and encourage a love of reading that will last a lifetime!

This edition first published in 2018 by Bellwether Media, Inc.

No part of this publication may be reproduced in whole or in part without written permission of the publisher. For information regarding permission, write to Bellwether Media, Inc., Attention: Permissions Department, 5357 Penn Avenue South, Minneapolis, MN 55419.

Library of Congress Cataloging-in-Publication Data

Names: Sommer, Nathan, author.
Title: Squids / by Nathan Sommer.
Description: Minneapolis, MN : Bellwether Media, Inc., [2018] | Series: Blastoff! Readers. Ocean Life Up Close | Audience: Age 5-8. | Audience: K to Grade 3. | Includes bibliographical references and index.
Identifiers: LCCN 2017028814 | ISBN 9781626177673 (hardcover : alk. paper) | ISBN 9781681034768 (ebook)
Subjects: LCSH: Squids–Juvenile literature.
Classification: LCC QL430.2 .S592 2018 | DDC 594/.58–dc23
LC record available at https://lccn.loc.gov/2017028814

Text copyright © 2018 by Bellwether Media, Inc. BLASTOFF! READERS and associated logos are trademarks and/or registered trademarks of Bellwether Media, Inc. SCHOLASTIC, CHILDREN'S PRESS, and associated logos are trademarks and/or registered trademarks of Scholastic Inc., 557 Broadway, New York, NY 10012.

Editor: Paige V. Polinsky   Designer: Brittany McIntosh

Printed in the United States of America, North Mankato, MN.

Table of Contents

What Are Squids?	4
Large Eyes and Soft Bodies	10
Capturing Prey	14
Squid Life	18
Glossary	22
To Learn More	23
Index	24

What Are Squids?

mantle

Caribbean reef squid

Squids are some of the world's largest **invertebrates**! They have huge **mantles** and large eyes.

Other Cephalopods

cuttlefish

octopuses

nautiluses

These **cephalopods** force water through their bodies to move. They can swim in any direction!

bigfin reef squid

Squids are found in every ocean. Most live at least 1,000 feet (305 meters) below the surface.

There is very little light so far down. But squids **adapt** to this **environment**. They can see far in the dark!

Squids come in many different sizes. The smallest are only about 0.6 inches (1.6 centimeters) long.

Squid Sizes

Smallest
southern pygmy squid

actual size

0.6 inches (1.6 centimeters) long

Largest
giant squid

average human

43 feet (13 meters) long

veined squid

southern pygmy squid

The largest are 43 feet (13 meters) long. These squids weigh nearly 1,000 pounds (454 kilograms)!

Large Eyes and Soft Bodies

The main part of a squid's body is called a mantle. Fins run along the top of it.

fin

eye

bobtail squid

A squid has large, round eyes below its mantle. **Pits** beneath the eyes help it smell.

tentacle

Eight arms and two **tentacles** help a squid move and grab food. These are covered with strong **suckers**.

A hard, pointy beak hides in the middle of a squid's long arms.

Identify a Squid

mantle | beak | tentacles

Capturing Prey

Squids are **carnivores** that hunt for their food. Fish, crabs, and shrimp are common **prey**.

Squids catch prey with their tentacles and bring it to their beaks. The beaks are strong enough to break through tough shells.

Catch of the Day

- Antarctic krill
- hermit crabs
- rockfish

Sea Enemies

sea otters

yellowfin tuna

orcas

Squid bodies are soft and easy for **predators** to eat. These cephalopods stay clear of hungry whales and tuna.

Some squids change colors to hide from danger. Others shoot out dark ink to confuse predators.

ink

Squid Life

Male squids interest females by changing colors quickly. Some males swim together in large circles while doing this.

eggs

Females lay many eggs at once. The eggs bunch together in long, jellylike tubes.

baby European squid

Baby squids **hatch** on the sea floor. They are on their own from the beginning.

These babies know how to swim right away. Soon, they will grow into strong sea predators!

Glossary

adapt—to become comfortable with something

carnivores—animals that only eat meat

cephalopods—animals that have excellent eyesight, ink sacs, and muscular arms with suckers; cuttlefish, octopuses, and squids are types of cephalopods.

environment—the features of a natural area

hatch—to break out of an egg

invertebrates—animals without backbones

mantles—folds of thick skin and muscle that make up the bodies of squids

pits—cells beneath the eyes of squids that help them smell

predators—animals that hunt other animals for food

prey—animals that are hunted by other animals for food

suckers—body parts that suck or cling

tentacles—long, bendable parts of a squid that are attached to the body and longer than the arms

To Learn More

AT THE LIBRARY

Derrick, David G., Jr. *Sid the Squid and the Search for the Perfect Job*. San Francisco, Calif.: Immedium, 2010.

Leaf, Christina. *Octopuses*. Minneapolis, Minn.: Bellwether Media, 2017.

O'Mara, John. *Red Devil Squid*. New York, N.Y.: Gareth Stevens Publishing, 2015.

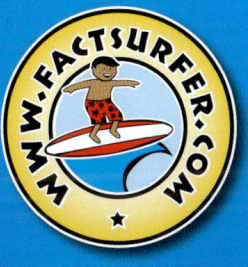

ON THE WEB

Learning more about squids is as easy as 1, 2, 3.

1. Go to www.factsurfer.com.

2. Enter "squids" into the search box.

3. Click the "Surf" button and you will see a list of related web sites.

With factsurfer.com, finding more information is just a click away.

Index

adapt, 7
arms, 12, 13
babies, 20, 21
beaks, 13, 14
bodies, 5, 10, 17
carnivores, 14
cephalopods, 5, 17
colors, 17, 18
depth, 6, 7
eggs, 19
eyes, 4, 11
females, 18, 19
fins, 10
food, 12, 14, 15
hatch, 20
hunt, 14
ink, 17
invertebrates, 4
life span, 7
males, 18
mantles, 4, 10, 11, 13
movement, 5, 12
pits, 11
predators, 16, 17, 21

prey, 14, 15
range, 6, 7
sizes, 4, 8, 9
status, 7
suckers, 12
swim, 5, 18, 21
tentacles, 12, 13, 14

The images in this book are reproduced through the courtesy of: Nature/UIG, front cover; Amanda Nicholls, pp. 3, 13 (top left); Mark Conlin/ Alamy, pp. 4-5; Rich Carey, pp. 5 (top), 13 (top right); magnusdeepbelow, p. 5 (center); atese, p. 5 (bottom); zaferkizilkaya, p. 6; Steve Bloom Images/ Alamy, p. 7; Reinhard Dirscherl/ Getty Images, p. 9 (top); Auscape/ Contributor/ Getty Images, p. 9 (bottom); Wolfgang Poelzer/ Getty Images, p. 10; optionm, p. 11; Narchuk, p. 12; Universal Images Group/ SuperStock, p. 13 (top center); John A. Anderson, p. 13 (bottom); Dmytro Pylypenko, p. 15 (top left); Petra Vavrova, p. 15 (top center); Joe Belanger, p. 15 (top right); Solvin Zankl/ Nature Picture Library, p. 15 (bottom); Png Studio Photography, p. 16 (top left); Shane Gross, p. 16 (top center); Andrea Izzotti, p. 16 (top right); Richard Whitcombe, p. 16 (bottom); FLPA/ Colin Marshall/ SuperStock, p. 17; National Geographic Creative/ Alamy, p. 18; Stocktrek Images, Inc./ Alamy, p. 19; Marevision/ age fotostock/ SuperStock, p. 20; YU YUN-PING, p. 21.